POEMS
And
SONGS

By
Will Pirone

Salem House Press
Salem, MA

Salem House Press
79 Bridge Street
Salem, MA 01970
And
1481 Newark Ave.
Whiting, N.J. 08759

All text copyright Will Pirone©
First Edition
Printed in U.S.

Some poems were published in school literary magazines at The American College of Switzerland and Salem State University. "Photos from the Family Album" appeared in Ploughshares in 1971, and is miraculously still online. "Baja Beach" and "Carnaval – La Paz appeared in "Baja Insider" in 2004. A few appeared in fly by night magazines and broadsides that vanished without a trace.

ISBN-10:   0983666563
ISBN-13:   978-0-9836665-6-1

LCCN: 2012934152

www.salemhousepress.com
Facebook: Salem House Press

POEMS

Cambridge mid sixties – The Road

Vermont Sunset	1
Strange Seasons	2
Love Song	4
Blues	5
Two Views of the Same Sunrise	6

San Francisco late sixties – The Street

Poem to Kathy	7
To Margie	7
Lazarus as the Ultimate Speed Freak	8
A Poem Which, the Title of Which…..	10
Grant Street: La Trieste	11
Jungian Love	12
Tides	13
Sixth and Market	13
The Great Mandala	14
To Those in Need of Song	18
The Idle Clock – Three Views	20
Photos from the Family Album	21
Implied Presence	22
Beatnik Hero	22

Los Angeles the eighties – The Boulevard

Chicago	23
Hot Day in Vermont	24
Ode to Jealousy and Rage	24
To a Woman M.B.A.	25
Lines Commemorating a Divorce	25
The Poet's Eye	26
Möbius #1	26
Möbius #2	26
Möbius 3.5 rev ii	27
Fragments Overheard in the Emergency Ward	28
Counterterrorism in Marina Del Rey	29
I Love L.A.	29
Cliché #3	29
Policeman's Nightmare	30
The Beach Police	31
Spring Stroll	32
Aesop's Haiku	32
The Book of Love	33
Fishing with the Telescope	34
The Man in the Moon	34
An Essay on Culture Bound Stereotypes	35
My Office Plant	36
The Key of C	36

Baja in the nineties – El Camino

The Redefinition of Joy	37
Baja Beach	38
Carnaval – La Paz	39
The Middle	40
The Bay of Illusion	41
Desert Dream	42

SONGS

Salem in the new millennium – The Common

Mr. Derby's Blues	**45**
Opening	**46**
The Bar Rag	**47**
Closing	**48**
Ballad of an F150	**49**
Gnostic Love Song	**50**
Frying Pan	**51**
Jukebox Kaleidoscope	**52**
Runners and Dreamers	**54**
Same Place, Different Life	**55**
Dream Box	**56**
Crippletown	**57**
Tim Leary's Jig (Is Up)	**58**
The Enlightenment Waltz	**59**
Sea of Despair	**60**
The Bipolar Blues	**62**
It Ain't Easy Being Old	**62**
The Pig's Eye Open Mike Subtext Shuffle	**63**
The Enlightenment Blues	**64**

INTRODUCTION

I was brought up to believe that the ability to write a poem is one of the accoutrements of a gentleman. It was the sole driver of my existence through my teens and early twenties. As an adult preoccupation, it gave perspective to my other pursuits.

The poems are in roughly chronological order. I have selected the ones I still like, and left them mostly as written. There are periods when I wrote very little, and times of failed experiments.

The selected ones fall into several periods: *The Road*, Cambridge in the mid sixties; *The Street*, San Francisco in the late sixties and Cambridge in the early seventies; *The Boulevard*, Los Angeles in the eighties; *El Camino*; Baja in the nineties.

The final section, *The Common,* Salem in the new millennium, is composed of songs. They were written as rhyming metric verse to make it easy to put them to music. In practice, the melodies arrived by the same mysterious route that the words took.

The earliest poems were written for two readings at Dudley House, Harvard University, in the spring of 1965. Some were published in school literary magazines at The American College of Switzerland and Salem State University. "Photos from the Family Album" appeared in Ploughshares in 1971, and is miraculously still online. "Baja Beach" and "Carnaval – La Paz" appeared in "Baja Insider" in 2004. A few appeared in fly by night magazines and broadsides that vanished without a trace.

Will Pirone
Salem 2012

Cambridge mid sixties – The Road

Vermont Sunset

Evenings violet afterglow
Streaks the Vermont mountain tops
And makes the road seem even flatter.
The road runs by the riverside,
Only a city block away
(But there are no cities here)
And even the river seems mundane
By ever present violet mountains.

Night comes and the road is dark
For no lights cut the afterglow
And new moon's unreflected shades
Have not yet risen to compete
With thunderous violent afterglow
That gives no light but seems to breathe
And spread in palpitating waves
From ever present twilight mountains.

The burning eyes of a passing car
Give a moments loss of vision;
In that moment comes the night,
With it dies the afterglow
As if it had been pulled away
And drowned within the blinding wake
Of moving headlights passing
Through ever present brooding mountains.

With sudden night comes quickened heartbeats
To bring forth sometimes latent fears
That bridge the twenty thousand years
Between the Vermont countryside
And prehistoric skin clad men
Frightened by the sudden dark,
Caught between the winding river
And ever present monstrous mountains.

Strange Seasons

When winter casts its still white shadow over spring
The dying city snowdrifts, like amoebas,
Wrap themselves around a dismal grain of sand,
And by some strange osmosis, find themselves consumed.

There is no joy in winter's early death
Crawling down the gutters toward the sea;
Spring is still some months away and miles south.
Winter may be dead, but windy ghosts haunt city streets.

A subtle nausea forces my escape
From this strange city season without name
That taunts me from the vacant alleyways
And shouts vague threats from gaping sewer grates.

Prompted by a magic seaborne breeze
I travel up the metamorphic coast
'Til Gloucester and the dunes of Wingaersheek
Come within a moment's view and hour's walk.

The summer houses, closed and vacant,
Cast ice cube shadows on pure snow.
I find a fieldstone house, set back from the point,
And sit down in its ice glazed breezeway.

Here the winter still remains alive and white
With drifts that run from dunes to high tide line
Extending gentle fingers to the water's edge
Where breakers stab the crystal beach

And carry off a grain of snow,
And carry in a grain of sand,
And leave behind strange hexagrams
Along the ripple crested flats.

No human step has ever touched these drifts,
The ridges stand like microscopic Rockies
With sculptured peaks and finely chiseled cliffs
That slope and stretch to coarser sand flat foothills.

It seems as if some ancient Chinese artist
Had made a brush consisting of three hairs
And with enchanted hands and gentle skill
Had spent a lifetime on this work of wind.

Upon the point a winter seabird stands
With spread wings and upturned beak,
Expectant and prepared for flight,
But for the moment strangely still.

It seems to be the ancient master's
Final brush stroke afterthought
Before he withered and became
A grain of snow entangled in a grain of sand.

Love Song

Love comes with unspoken words
And is accepted in a touch
Of hands or unasserted glance
That is conceived in question
And answered with a smile.

It almost seems as if the word
Were some strange occidental form
Of OM, the mystic syllable,
Which loses power once it's said.

This word also, left unspoken,
First in unsure expectation,
Then in unsaid certitude,
Builds its magic in its silence.

But too often, first expression
Comes with threats or subtle pleas
After harsher words have broken
The magic built in silent spells.

Then indeed, I think it best
That lovers never speak at all,
(What use have they of words?)
A kiss dies cold on speaking lips.

Blues

The sunrise seemed much brighter then,
In warm of spring and summer rains
With clearer nights and streetlight stars.
But autumn brought the fallen leaves
With thoughts of still the echoed smile
And blacker eyes and raven hair
Drifting on a gentle breeze.

But the leaves fell in a green rain,
And passed through azogrenadine
Then resolved themselves in gold.
The snow fell on the loneliness
Of newer loses with remorse
For bluer eyes and golden hair
Floating on a ray of light.

The blue and icy spears must fall
From tightened wires and stiffened poles
Stabbing virgin drifts and fertile soil.
But with the thaws of spring come thoughts
Of winter's latest harsh defeats
And greener eyes and auburn hair
Swirling on a wandering mistral.

With bitter spring comes solitude,
The flowers blooming dead and brown
Fall like black neglected harvests
In a raped and conquered land
And lead to half remembered thoughts
Of blacker, bluer, greener eyes,
And raven, golden, auburn hair
Stagnant in miasmic downpours
Seen in a schizophrenic landscape
By sunset's bleeding rain clouds.

Two Views of the Same Sunrise

I

The ancient god Apollo
Now grown old and growing blind
Hides his sole cycloptic eye
Behind a gauze of waxen clouds.

An old man in a white muffler,
He takes his routine morning stroll
Through misty winter downtown streets.

I wonder why he even bothers,
His only other audience,
A jaundiced light bulb in an attic
Staring past the shrouded rooftops.

II

This morning is a grey dawn
That comes with over cautious steps
As if resentful of the sky.

The weary late-night-morning sun,
Newly frightened by its task,
Lurks behind the harbingers
Of somewhere else's snowstorm.

The birds' uncertain silences
Punctuate spasmodic cries;
They cannot hide in leafless trees.

San Francisco late sixties – The Street

Poem to Kathy

I think that I have seen her face but once,
And then not in a dream that morning kills,
Or rather simply chooses not to show.

For had I only seen her in a dream
I would not face her sleeping form
At dawn when dreams have lost their truth.

A face that casts a shadow not its own
Is sometimes really not a face at all,
Forgotten in the face that morning shows,
But just a ghost that comes to haunt our days
And flood the dreadful landscape of our dreams
By simply not appearing.

To Margie

I would have written love songs,
Sung them to the hills,
Embedded them in trees
Among the stolen images of God.

But then I lost my song
To the closeness of love.

The panting rhythm grows
Crescendos
Goes.

Most gladly
Love song
Lost
To the bedspring's truer rhyme
That catches the breath of a dream.

Lazarus as the Ultimate Speed Freak

The man in the blue hat walks
Down the diamond studded street
Amid the shouts of barkers
      that he never hears.
"Step right up, ladies and gentlemen,
Step right up, some of the best entertainment
On Broadway; tastes just like a peanut butter
Sandwich."

Meanwhile the troglodyte
Looks up foreboding sewer grates
And wonders at the glitter of the streets
Above,
Sees the blue hat and shouts,
"Lazarus!   Lazarus!
Where are you now that we need you?"
Is spotted by the diamond in his eye
And retreats back to the underground
Before the blue hat spins on his heel
Kicking diamond rays here and away;
Freaks:
"Lazarus, you mother-fucker,
I'll get you yet, and when I do
I'll kill your ass for good
This time."

Lazarus laughs:
"Blah-blah-blah-blah-blah"
At the blue hat jack boot Jackass
And retreats back into the gutter
Shoots up under a manhole cover
Then shoots up   from   under a manhole cover
And raps down the diamond studded street
Behind the blue hatted et cetera:
"I'm Lazarus, I tell you, Lazarus
Come back from the dead,
Come to tell you all."

The blue hat busts him,
 Don't believe him.
Just another street-freak speed-freak.

"I thought," he says (or rather raps)
"I thought that coming out of heaven
(What a flash!   What a flash!)
That in the aftermath, at least,
I could dream of heaven.
But no   damn-it   no
Not only did I didn't die,
I didn't even sleep no more,
And soon the memory,
These nineteen hundred years or so
Has faded."

"Sure, sure," the blue hat says
And dumps him in the cell to kick.

Poor Lazarus, now,
These nineteen hundred years of unbelieving cops and such,
Is truly,
And with reason,
Paranoid.

A little Thorazine will slow him down, they think,
And sure enough;
It did.

But then,
Going out on the nod
He wondered
As he remembered it (so well)
If heaven were not
A crystal palace,
With needle spires.

A Poem Which, the Title of Which, and the Location and the Author, at the Time, All Being Different Uses of the Same Word, That Being the First Word of the Poem……..

High
On Tamalpais
Daring blindness
Beyond the trees....
Quivering on a sunbeam
My burned body
Fused to the green grass
By the sun's heliac arc
And the acid catalyst……….

But as I was saying before the

      FLASH!

I looked down on the city
A spreading cancer
On the lush green peninsula……..
Coming down and going home
Was much like falling down the microscope
And finding on closer inspection
That my analogy
Was right . . . . . .

Grant Street: La Trieste

Ah, yes,
He sits in La Trieste
Hustling a freckle-faced girl
In a polka dotted mini dress,
Rapping his line
And trying to score.

She, still attentive arid bright eyed,
Stifles a yawn, and studies his line.

She's heard it all a million times before.

The hustler won't get laid,
And knows it too,
But won't admit that he plays
For love   of the game.
The smell of warm thighs
Echoes too firmly
In the moonlit alleys
Of his mind.

Jungian Love

"The meeting of two personalities is like the contact of two chemical substances: if there is any reaction both are transformed." Jung

Fission.
The smell of an empty room
Where love was made
Ago.
The echo of their voices   laughter
Just out of sight
That slowly settles into silence
Like a lonely man
Upon his once more solitary bed.

While far beyond the universe's edge
Atoms collide at random,
Rebound or bind,
And a laughing god regards
With equal eye
The transformations
Of his play things.

Tides

Old men see with infant's eyes,
Their distance from the shores of time   the same,
Simplicity of truth upon them lays his hands
To show that ocean's depth with wisdom born of knowledge.

The wrinkles of an old man's face display
The imprint of the palm of time made clear;
Life chooses lines from deep primordial stores
As sea winds etch our common wave born fate.

For infants, like old men, are wrinkle draped;
As a dying man's last sigh escapes the void
To fill the newborn baby's gasping lungs,
The backhand slap of death rebounds to form
The open hand that spanks the spark of life.
For wrinkle lines, the infant's ancient eyes
Are but the changing waves upon the ocean's face.

Sixth and Market

San Francisco: New Years Eve.
On the way home from the party
We drive by Sixth at Market Street
And watch the old winos,
Sedentary on the curbstone,
Like so many stark shadows
Or lost and abandoned
Christmas trees.

The Great Mandala

I
The Children's Crusade
In our first days of vagabondage
With neither star nor pillar guiding
Wandered we beneath the shadow,
Bear-like, ever turning, by black castle keeps.
All wandered we, a generation lost,
No guide but Peter, holy hill born hermit.
No Pope or king could stop our marching
As each one bore his own true cross
To free Jerusalem.

To sea we went, Atlantis fearing not,
Nor off the sea edge falling,
Ever turning in our quest,
The center of our universe, the Holy Tree;
And each one toward that cross was turning.
Like spreading spokes of the moving wheel
                we came
Following the shadow of the Virgin
Rising with the sun to catch the moon
In arms of night and labyrinths of day.

As we wandered, rivers followed, Rhine and Rhone,
High towers did their dark watch keep,
Their children prisoners as we passed
To only find them later lost
Toward that high hill that knows no shadows
Where all horizons stop,
                      we wandered.

And lost we many on the way:
Some to vagabondage lost
Some to home returned too soon
Some to slavery sold by Sodom
And some to the stomach of the sea.
Returned not many from their questing
Nor many found the hub's still center,
Mostly wandered by the rivers
Turned by wheel spokes never ceasing
Down to labyrinths of ocean
Lost beyond Atlantis sea edge
Their call to arms become a plea
Their crosses all grown heavy now
By ever darkening castle keeps
And slipped beyond the shadow ever seeking
'Til starless night that knows no turnings
Released us all from vagabondage
              lost.

II

The Five Meditations of the Hermit
I have marked out my life in the rhythm of trees
That have long since passed to the spinning of time,
Itself to be lost in the breath of leaves dropping,
Recircling, cease falling as time slowly turns,
And so turning falls, the leaf still suspended.

First on horizons harsh travels I charted
Losing my way to the spinning of stars.
Only by stopping between the still centers
Did I fathom the subtle symmetrical eye
Whose circle reverses the cycle of night.

Sand being lifted falls limpid again
Nor can wind by its sighing give breath to the beach
As seas with their churning left life on the shore.
But grass turns its blade between sands rippled ribs
In search of the source that defines it from dirt.

Sky coupling clouds in their whimsical flight
Tempt birds from their task of defining the curve
Of horizons that touch on the arms of the sea;
Years I have watched them from nest to nest
Repeating the circle, denying the curve.

Wind whips like lashes in a blink of time
As the sun looks down through a funnel of clouds.
From the hurricane's eye is imagined a face
Whose lips form a sound from the storm's silent hub
That quietly calls in the space between heartbeats.

III
The Vision
I pass along the labyrinth
Of San Francisco city streets
Up Grant
Beyond Vallejo.
The bottle passes
Hand to hand
Around the circle.
On its upward turn
It catches streetlight stars,
Returns to shrouded figures
In dark doorways.

"Acid? Grass? Hash?
Spare change, Brother?

The city screams from the mouth
Of Telegraph Hill.
I walk by barrooms;
Laughter shrieks within.

At Grant and Green
Another bottle passes
Around the quiet circling hands
Like the moving center
Of a lost wheel.

An old man approaches down the hill,
A hermit from Coit's tower.
"Are you ready, Brother, Are you ready?
The end is near."

I pass silently and know
Apocalypse will come on rubber wheels
The horsemen dressed in blue
Their hooves the sound of clinking cuffs
Their mounts spewing tear gas.
For I have seen the vision
On my hill.
High above the city
By Coit's Tower
I have dreamed and watched
The rising sun's first rays
Release the leaves from darkness
One by one
As even it reveals
The fallen tower's ribs.

And I have dreamed
And seen
Three boats
Beyond the ruins of the bridge,
Its golden sunrise glow
Turned red
With whipping sea brined cables.

Three boats,
I say,
At the harbor's mouth
Their sails ripped
And rippling in the wind.

Three boats spinning
Around the whirlpool's rim
Pulling toward the hub
Of New Atlantis.

To Those in Need of Song

Screams   Bells   Running feet.
The people stood in clusters
Staring at the scene.

The Emperor watched from the balustrade.
We are told that he fiddled,
Although the press denied the story
In the public interest
And blamed the whole affair
On the Christians
Or the Jews.

It all depends upon which fire we choose;
Rome or the Reichstag.
The details of the place and people,
Even of which man or myth
Are much the same.

The next day people watched
Gestapo agents round them up.

In the Coliseum, the Emperor was upset.
Some man (the press did not report has name),
Rumor calls him Simon, code named Peter,
A Jew or Christian, again,
Depending on which fire you have in mind;
But anyway,
Before he could be apprehended,
He led the condemned in song,
A hymn, perhaps a Kaddish
Punctuated by screams
Or running feet
And bells when the gas went on.

The Emperor judged the man himself.
When the sentence   Crucifixion
Was handed down
The prisoner's only comment was,
"No better way
Than in the footsteps
Of my Lord."

They hung him upside down.
I have often wondered at his thoughts
And may have seen a man who might have known.
Enlightenment, I have been told
Arrives in flashes.

"We interrupt this game
To bring you a special news report
Hot from the wires of U.P.I. "

The scene was brief
The commentator's words forgotten
There were no bells or running feet
Nor was there any singing:
Just a small bald man
(His name was not reported).
Who baptized himself with gasoline
And lit it.

The Idle Clock – Three Views

I

Beneath the clock's perpetual noon
The children play in the shadowless room.

I am a simple man Lord,
My life is but child's play
And I am but a child
At play with other children.

In the light of other mornings
I have thoughts of other children
Asleep in other rooms.

II

The frozen clock releases me.
Idle thoughts and necessary truths
Are equally caught on its upturned hands.
Here we measure time by empty glasses.

III

The clock's relentless midnight stance
Denies the truth of three A.M.
"I want to be alone" the lady says.

Later
In another room
Alone
I watch the sunrise
Thinking necessary thoughts
Made complex by the time between
Conception and fruition.

Truth is so much simpler,
A timeless child
I bounce upon my knees.

Photos from the Family Album

Random frames from the flow of time
Are dealt like hands of solitaire
Or perhaps a fortune being told.
An unknown woman in Victorian dress
Is sitting, back turned, by a lake,
Blond hair across her shoulder;
A cat drinks water from a tap.
The smiling faces of strangers and friends
Arrange themselves in no strict order;
My great grandfather in his youth
Sits beside his ancient son.

I dream of her often:
The lady by the lake.
The image becomes general,
Any lady by a lake will do.
A cat drinking from a tap.

The photos fall like yarrow sticks.
My father's quick smile passes
Beneath the question in his eyes
Like wind over water,
His father looking much the same,
Perhaps a little like myself.
The image becomes general.

My grandfather's pictures are set aside,
On top a formal portrait at my age.
I see his long body in my own;
I often feel him in the morning
When I stretch and seek my lover,
Blond hair across her shoulder.
Identity is found in both directions:
Both in the cat and in the tap
From which he drinks.

Implied Presence

The Egyptians had the right idea.
Isis, their goddess of creation,
Was an irresistible whore;
This age cannot appreciate
The beauty of that concept.

I watched her at work in the park today.
People ignored her in much the same way
That they did not see the two dogs.

Beatnik Hero

He was among the truly free,
That is, the poor
Who needn't be.

Los Angeles the eighties – The Boulevard

Chicago

City of Siberian winds
Blown past the pole
By Alaskan highs.

In Arapaho
I think it means
Brown stones
On the flat land
Beside the stagnant water.

Three years there
Was like time served;
Please don't send me to Gorki.
I promise not to write
Political poems
Anymore.

Hot Day in Vermont

The sky looked like triple dips
Of chocolate and maple walnut;
There will be thunder on the river
Later on tonight. But now
The only threat is from
The open mouths of covered bridges.

Oral fixations abound
In the verse of prior times;
Darwin makes me simian
Above White River Junction,
And as for Freud ---

My favorite Vermont postcard shows,
Amid the burning maple leaves,
The open lips on ancient bridgework,
And beyond
The rounded mounds of mountains
Like double scoop banana splits
Beneath the whipped cream sky.

Ode to Jealousy and Rage

No matter how you paint the feeling,
Red or green,
It hardens to a hue
That always comes out blue.

To a Woman M.B.A.

The seamless surface cannot hide
The strain behind the smile.
The corporate culture value set
Has lost a vital file.

The equation fails to balance
When love is at the root
Of the present value/future value
Ratio you compute.

Lines Commemorating a Divorce

It started off
Like a pleasant dream
Until around the corner
Or climbing the stair
We meet the monster.

On waking I remember
That it had a face like ours:
That is like yours and mine.
Perhaps it is the child
We never had.

The Poet's Eye

The mirrored möbius triptych of my mind
Reflects upon itself (itself, itself)
While all who peer within
See some distorted image
They've projected.

It's just a funhouse
Hall of mirrors;
Attenuated ego
Convex superego
Leaded smoky id.

Möbius #1

How like our love;
Birds in adjacent cages
Preen and strut
Never commenting
On the bars between them
Until they seem no longer there:
How like two birds
In adjacent cages.

Möbius #2

All former loves invading dreams
Assume the Aphrodite guise,
Moist lips, deep eyes, the open womb
(The truth is never what it seems.)

While in another empty space
Another fantasy takes place
Until at last awake we face
The vacant mirrored room.

Möbius 3.5 rev ii

The memo of the mind rewrites itself
Conceiving of itself as being written.
It is a passive thing. It never thinks
Of writer, reader but of
'It has been written'
'It has been read'
'The committee thinks'
'The staff had thought.'

The id gets fucked
Conceiving of itself as getting laid.
It is a passive aggressive thing. It never
Thinks of anything
But itself.
The committee thinks it ought to go away.
The staff had thought that it had come.

She lay there
Looking up into his face
Wondering why she saw a double image:
One eye blue,
One black,
The third one missing.

Fragments Overheard in the Emergency Ward

I
'The Blood Test'

Doc, I know you think
The pesticide and fertilizer come
From what I'm smoking.
But if I was you
I'd keep away
From fruits and vegetables,
Like me.

II
'The Overdose'

So after we pumped his stomach out
And loaded him full of saline,
He began to come around.
Groggy at first, he mumbled,
'Who's got the dope?'
Then, fully aware of his surroundings
He pulled the catheter out and screamed,
'You mother fuckers blew my high.'

III
'The Killer'

I always hate it when they say,
'The killer struck with surgical precision.'
They never say,
'The doctor sliced him up and down and
Cut his ass 'til he was wasted.'
They both are here, all bloody,
Avoiding each other's eyes.

Counterterrorism in Marina Del Rey

They cannot fool me with
Their talk of freedom
I hear the helicopters
Every night.

I Love L.A.

I have become an Angelino,
Afraid of empty spaces.
It's not so much the fear of openness
As fear of being caught on foot
At night
Alone.

Meat on the rack……….
The streets of Venice….
Flashing cars…………...
Agoraphobic dancers….

Cliché #3

She was a real gem
A multifaceted personality.
Sometimes you got a mirror
Sometimes a lens.
Perhaps a small flaw
Endlessly repeated
Or sudden flash
Of brilliance.

Policeman's Nightmare

In a police state
Even the cops
Are afraid.

They wake up sweating
When predawn prowls
Of cat or dog or man emit
The sound of three fast knocks.

In that long moment
Even they await the shout:
Police Warrant!
Police Warrant!
Police Warrant!
Before the door comes down.

And wonder what good buddy,
Pro,
Or con,
Has cut a deal
Behind their scam;
Then take the fall
To fitful sleep.

The Beach Police

Their aquamarine polo shirts
And navy blue bermudas
May be beach,
But the S&M dream belt
Is strictly cop.

They cruise the strand
On Schwinns and Raleighs
Repossessed to pay back fees
Or seized to prove conspiracy
In three joint, two kid beach busts.

A ludicrous police state microcosm
Until the schizophrenic beggar falls
Mingling blood, bullets, mire, and muscatel.

The headlines read:
BOUND AND NAKED PCP ABUSER SHOT
ATTEMPTING TO OVERPOWER POLICE
ON VENICE BOARDWALK YESTERDAY.
ACCOMPLICE ESCAPES
BY STEALING DETECTIVE'S
UNMARKED TRICYCLE.

Spring Stroll

Habitual upward glance in passing
Just meets averted downward gaze.
It has the sense of steps receding
Down a long and echo-laden hall
(That is all).

Brushing past the blossoms
In the planter by your door
I feel a fragment from a future life
When I will catch the trace of your perfume
As aromatic swirls in your retreat.

Head tilted back to hold its fading bloom
I close my eyes and see you smiling down
Then notice that it is your favorite scent,
"La Balconade" by Countess Juliette
(Not yet).

Aesop's Haiku

The fable of
The grasshopper and the ant:
       I am the butterfly.

The Book of Love (Cliché #4)

My heart is an open book
Albeit, somewhat dog-eared.
I will tell you about
The missing pages
If you do not ask about
The ones inserted in their place.

They all are there for you to browse,
Even the list that starts 'Dream on.'
As for the burns, they don't go through
More than a penciled page or two.

Those last few pages, scribbled on,
Are carbons where the ink bled through
When the book was closed and kept from sight.
But the following page is clean and white.

Fishing with the Telescope

A terrestrial fisherman uses the moon
As celestial bait in the telescopes eye.
The moon in his mirror seems closer to him
Than the one that the sea is reflecting.

A mercurial maiden shuts off her TV
And walks by the ocean to wish on a star,
But the spherical lure on the fisherman's line
Draws her close to his still, waiting figure.

She approaches him slowly, more slowly he turns,
And wordlessly offers a magnified view;
She is drawn down the lens to the inverted orb
While he's drawn to the one in the ocean.

They imagine each other as drawn to that place
By coincidence, not the sky's turning.
In a trance they are joined as their lines of sight meet
And are caught in the moon's net of yearning.

The Man in the Moon

I have seen the man in the moon
One eye in darkness, one in light
Head turned slightly to the left
Tilted slightly to the right.
No chin, no brow
As if peering down a microscope
Or through a reflex camera.

His time must run
Less quickly than our own;
The shutter clicks so slowly.

An Essay on Culture Bound Stereotypes

At first she seemed to me
Like all my green-eyed
Aunts and cousins.
.
Girl of my dreams
Woman of my fantasies
Lady of my public life
Resolve into the witch of nightmare.

(In the whitewashed medieval hill town of my father's birth
The perpetual widow sweeps dust from her husband's grave.
His photo on the headstone looks uncomfortably like me.)

Voluptuous hag
Sparred spread and sag
But not time's wrinkles;
You did not remind me
Of aunts and cousins
Until the not so instant replay
Of all my dreams and fantasies
Slo-moed voiceless frame by frame
Into that most familiar clip
Of green-eyed confrontation.

It will resolve to the beach at Malibu
Where the gum commercial blond
With the computer enhanced tan
Will remind me in a voice
That does not mirror
The cadence of the neighborhood
That this is the segue
From the part I call
"The why I live
In California
Blues."

My Office Plant

My plant,
An early gift
We thought might thrive
In windowless fluorescent fields,
Is dying.

It has
A better chance
Than we do here
Beneath the strobe eclipse
Of bar code L.A. love light.

The Key of C

The woman playing the stringless guitar
Hears every note.
Look into her eyes
You too
May catch a passing phrase.

Baja the nineties – El Camino

The Redefinition of Joy

Morning sun through stained glass windows
Splashes gold leaf plaster with glass mosaic

Red streaks through a stylized martyr's robe
Descend the chancel wall beside the cross

Turquoise water crimson blood
Stream from the unpierced Icon's side.

Below the living voice proclaims its joy
In the song of a hundred of His members.

Baja Beach

The cirrostratus clouds assemble
Pixel-like against the blue screen sky.
Why does the angry Aztec god appear
Shaking his white feathered headdress?

Twelve gnarled desert bushes
Mutely observe from the beach side bluff.
Exposed roots weave a blanket frieze
Across the cliff's eroded strata.

They do not acknowledge my wave.

The skeletons of little fish
are strewn like curled brown leaves
Beside the upturned boat
At the dry river's mouth.

We recline in its shadow.

The striped banner of beach and sea and sky
Hardly flutters to the wave's white noise;
A tiny mollusk sucks sand inside a tide washed shell,
While cantilevered shrimp boats strain to draw their catch
Across the far horizon's all encompassing edge.

Carnaval – La Paz

The iridescent abalone shell sky
Is sunset's backdrop to paradise.
Silhouette masts comb the clouds
While the big screen whoosh and creak
Of a yacht race fills the sound track.

Cowboy sailors see visions of freedom
Vikings fulfill genetic dreams.
The modem crackles
The cockfight cackles
The line is drawn
And is gone.

The sybaritic dance goes on.

The one day past new moon
Sits like an upraised cup
Above the sand spit strand.
It tips and disappears
As night's shell snaps.

The cue ball hits the pack
The carbon mast shatters
The dance is all that matters.
Stragglers with noisemakers pause
For a final anemic screech.
The eight ball drops.

The Middle

Between the bar and the door
The embrace and the release
Lies the moment of truth
Where the truth has escaped.

Retrograde mercury
Moon four days from full

The empty street.
The barking dog.

The Bay of Illusion

Our Lady of perpetual sorrows
Sits on the lawn by the church.
There are not enough tears in the world
To fill up the hole in her heart.

Her planet's lunar cycle has thirteen weeks.
The moons orbit is egglike, elliptic and long.

Black rock looming
In the noonday sky
The world awash
In tides and tears.

Six weeks later
The distant glowing smudge
Hides in the darkness
Above a placid sea.

At each extreme
She sings her song:

Love found,
Love betrayed.
Love lost,
Not made.
It comes;
It goes.

It has death throes.

Desert Dream

In the Vizcaino desert at dawn
I dream a New England day
Low sun pale in the brittle sky
A town common's snowfield
Crusted to the granularity of sand.

Dormant tree trunks reach
Like giant saguaro cactus
Inverse fork with bent
Broken tines imploring.

Branches extend shoots
Iced into spiny thorns
Thrust at motionless air.

SONGS

"You want to make sure no one reads your stuff?"
Publish it in a literary journal.
"You want to get heard?"
Write a song and sing it.

Salem in the New Millennium – The Common

Mr. Derby's Blues

Standing with my back against the lighthouse
Looking back along the ancient quay
Breezes run like skiffs across the harbor
The evening chill says autumn's on the way.

I still miss you, darling, as I missed you then
When spotlights lit the custom house each night
And back-lit lovers walked along the pathway
And I was first alone and things weren't right.

When nothing works I seem to wander back here
And walk the long since darkened wharf at night.
It's long years since we each have left this city.
I'm still alone and things are still not right.

Opening

Went to the bar the other night
To catch a tune or two.
The last thing I expected
Was that I'd run into you.

Always pleasant, always kind,
We'd often pass a word or two.
Somewhat quiet, self contained,
Sometimes a touch of blue.

Leave me an opening
And you know I will come through
Leave me an opening
And I will open up to you.

Perhaps it was the melody,
Perhaps the wine and beer.
Unguarded conversation
Let the misconceptions clear.

Reality is often just
Projected hopes and fears
Politeness merely shields us
From the world of joy and tears.

Leave me an opening
And you know I will come through
Leave me an opening
And I will open up to you.

We'll make room enough for two.

The Bar Rag

Listen to your better angel
The one who drinks.
You've been spending too much time
With the one who thinks.
You've got me thinking thoughts enough
To fill the minds of two.
Why don't you come out tonight
And join me for a few.

The conversation flows along
The band picks up the beat.
We catch last call and talk some more
Then take it to the street.
We do better 'round midnight
Than most lovers do
Though all I ever seem to get
Is a hug and peck from you.

Listen to your better angel
The one who drinks.
You've been spending too much time
With the one who thinks.
The message that is coming
Through the music in the night
Is that the one who thinks, pays for the drinks
But the one who drinks is right.

Closing

The little stab wound near my heart
I sterilize with alcohol.
I sign your name to clear the tab,
But in the end I pay it all.

Tiny sutures close the wound,
They say it will not leave a scar.
"X"es stitched with a poet's pen
On a post card sent from a tourist bar.

The next time hit me in the face.
It's easy, do it with a kiss,
The kind that I can really feel.
I will not move; you cannot miss.

The little stab wound near my heart
I sterilize with alcohol.
It stings a bit, but I don't mind.
It's better than no heart at all.

Ballad of an F150

The road is not a metaphor
In someone else's song
It is part of the life I lead,
The place where I belong.

Solitary, clear, direct.
Wheel on the road and in my hand.
At eighty miles an hour
My truck becomes my band.

White lines call the cadence out
Radials slap the bass
Harmonic doppler melodies
And I am in my place.

LA, Boston, Mexico
Destination is not goal
The existential question
Is forgotten as I roll.

(I wrote this song for all my friends
Who play here at the Pig.
I'll see you all in seven weeks
If I don't get a gig.)

Gnostic Love Song

We think that love is like our human heart
Elastic, strong yet fragile, beating true
A shifting lattice screen we're drawn to watch
But often are reluctant to pass through.

And on the other side
What is it that we hide?
Our passion and our pride
Disguised as doubt
We must work out.

But love is really never like a heart
Unless we count the Valentine of lace
With two symmetric sides we fold and cut
Then turn into a fan to shield our face.

And on the other side
What is it that we hide?
Attraction undenied
Disguised as fate.
We hesitate.

So love is like a poem or a song
That uninvited fills the artist's heart
Which seems to have existed all along
As if dictated by a soul apart.

And on the other side
What is it that we hide?
Love felt but not yet tried
Disguised as art.
Let's trust our heart.

Frying Pan

Like a chorus in my mind I know that you will come around
To fill my head with thoughts both pink and blue.
The pink is for the décor of your kitchen
The blue is for the heart that once loved you.

We used to sit at your formica table
To talk and sing the way old lovers do.
There never seemed to be a lack of topics
But then, we never spoke of me and you.

The Regulator ticks away an hour
The microwave display writes off the day
The empty rosé bottle on the table
Says that it's time for me to fade away.

I know I could have left you in the morning
And watched the sun put shadows on your sheets
But times have changed, and so have we, my darling
And so it's from the kitchen to the streets.

Jukebox Kaleidoscope

My living room has got a wheel
That I can lay my head down on
And mourn the passing of another day.
The picture window curves a bit
The truckbed bedroom's a tight fit
The hallway mirror faces the wrong way.

The coffee table opens up
Between me and the other chair
The place you used to read and sit and snooze.
You used to run the stereo
And play sweet love songs as we'd go
But now it's either silence or the blues

It's my jukebox kaleidoscope
My rolling video game
The world spins 'round me like a carousel.
It used to be my happy home
My concert hall, my pleasure dome,
But now it's just my lonely hermit's cell.

Kansas still is flat they tell me
Colorado still is high.
The deserts still are hot, the mountains cold.
I've seen them all and will again
And places I've not been
But now this life is getting kind of old.

I'll sell the truck and get a car
Rent a place and buy some stuff
And wonder how I ever lived that way.
A new true love will come along
We'll find another favorite song
And in a while they both will go away.

I'll go out on the sea next time
A new jukebox kaleidoscope
I'll turn the wheel and watch the ocean swell.
I'll joke about my happy home
Sing songs 'bout how I love to roam
And try and tell myself it's just as well.

It's my jukebox kaleidoscope
My rolling video game
The world spins 'round me like a carousel.
It used to be my happy home
My concert hall, my pleasure dome,
But now it's just my lonely hermit's cell.

Runners and Dreamers

Dreamers have to dream, that's who they are.
Runners have to run, that's what they do.
They really aren't that different deep inside,
Their mirrored sunglass soul stares back at you.

No matter what you dream or where you run
How little or how much you leave or pack
You'll still be there inside you when you stop
You'll still have that same baggage on your back.

It's only in your mind
And that's a scary thought.
You always bring the part
You wish that you'd forgot.

Sisyphus has got his rock to push.
The runners and the dreamers know their role
All three are on a journey that repeats
And so confuse the process with the goal.

The runner dreams of running in the night
The dreamer runs his dreamscapes through the day
The runner stops at dawn to dream of love.
The dreamer dreams of love and runs away.

It's only in your mind
And that's a scary thought.
You always leave the part
You shouldn't have forgot.

Same Place, Different Life

What is it that you don't recall?
A foolish question on its face.
Was it an echo in the song?
A prior life, a similar place?

We sat and heard this melody
As ancient as the space we share.
The same colonial sitting room,
Do you remember we were there?

Or here, it's really all the same
The song, the mood, the hint of dawn.
We wondered what would happen next
And in a while we both were gone.

In this life, not the next or last
It doesn't have to end that way.
We each remember differently,
And then we both decide to stay.

Dream Box

Escape the box. It's made of dreams.
It's not as solid as it seems.
"In love with" means that there are two
Bet there is no one here with you.

A dream should ease you through the night
But then should fade into the light.
The nightmare says "get out of here."
Your own true voice is what you fear.

There is a box that you can see
Turn upside down and wind the key
It plays a pretty song…
About a dream gone wrong…

Yes it plays a pretty song…
About a dream gone wrong…

The clockwork ballerina spins
In circles never ending.
Her skates have cracked the mirrored lake
That hides what she's defending.

But it plays a pretty song…
About a dream gone wrong…

"Beautiful dreamer, wake unto me"
Repeats with pace descending.
The song runs down. The dancer stops.
At last one dream is ending.

Escape the box. It's made of dreams.
It's not as solid as it seems.
"In love with" means that there are two.
But there's no dancer here with you.

Two boxes side by side are swept
From Shiva's workbench table top.
One built by hand, one made of dreams,
Aligned by fate, they merge and drop.

Distant dreamers share a song
They dance and part in fitful sleep.
At dawn they hear the fading tune.
Clockwork dancer starts to weep.

Crippletown

Trappings and Baggage, fresh wounds and deep scars
Come sit down beside me in these downtown bars
The silence is easy when inside each mind
Are meanings to lyrics that the author can't find.

They come and they stay for a month or a year
Wondering how they have ended up here.
Crippletown needs you, come join in our game
We recall your story, but rarely your name.

The details are different, they all end the same
The lies, the abuse, then the feelings of shame.
Everyone struggles beneath a veneer
That slowly dissolves when it's polished with beer

So sit down beside me and tell me again
The trouble you've had and the names of the men.
Each time it gets deeper and closer to true
Each time I get drawn a bit closer to you.

In the lost and found the unmatched mittens pray
That someone with wit or some art will come stay.
I always go home to that same lonely bed
There's one like the others; "no" was all that she said.

Tim Leary's Jig (Is Up)

At Abu-Gharib and Guantanamo Bay
All the guards were reservists from jail towns up state
What's been happening there has been happening here
So how different are we from the tyrants we hate?

All the news that I watch on my TV is trite
It's celebrity trials or a poor person's grief,
A publicity stunt, or a planted sound bite.
What the press fails to show is beyond my belief.

Where is the truth? What don't we see?
It looks like a lie to me.

So they give us loose credit, too good to decline,
Then they jack up the interest until it's a squeeze
Use your inflated house for an equity line
That turns short debt to long, while they skim off their fees.

Read directions completely, then turn upside down.
Don't inhale the propellant, shake well before use.
Change the bankruptcy laws and we'll take back the town
While we start a campaign to fight credit abuse.

Where are our values? Why can't we see?
It looks like a scam to me.

Both the Bushes are Yalies, and Kerry's one too,
With their secret society preppie elites
Also Lieberman, Clinton, to name just a few.
It's an oligarch's dream, no election defeats.

A republicrat candidate wins every race.
They will mouth the same lies that they're all told to tell.
The police state, the war, and the cash stay in place
While we argue about who will lead us to hell.

Who is the patriot? Where can he be?
It looks like a crime to me.

A hit before breakfast relaxes the mind
And helps you to deal with the day that's ahead.
The puritans hate it, but their world's a grind
So I live in my own, where I'm happy, instead.

The hypocrites rule and the parasites thrive.
What passes for normal looks real strange to me.
I try to ignore them and still stay alive
In the home of the slave and the land of the flea.

Where is the liberty? Who's really free?
It looks like a trap to me.
Don't call Homeland Security.
They've got plenty of pictures of me.

The Enlightenment Waltz

There's times I'm aware of the world that's outside
And sometimes I'm probably not.
Reality's been overrated, I'm told
We mostly project what we're taught.

Look deep in yourself for a moment or two
See who else is living inside
Then banish them all, 'til you have but one voice
And that one has no place to hide.

Just quiet that voice and you'll still be right there
In a silent and shimmering space
Where love is abundant and peace is profound
And you're one with the whole human race.

So stifle your ego and sit on your id
Just think of the damage they do.
Get rid of your self, it's a burden at best,
And seek out the spirit in you.

Sea of Despair

She came to you softly, and kind
Looking for some peace of mind
But you weren't quite ready
Your feet weren't too steady
She missed what she wanted to find

It's probably in there somewhere.
Down under that sea of despair
You ought to go find it
And try to unbind it
And let it come up for some air.

She came back for a second look
And read you like an open book
But the binding was shattered
The pages got scattered
And the index was all that she took

It's probably in there somewhere
And could be rewritten with care
You ought to go find it
And try to rebind it
And save it from such disrepair.

So now she's around but unsure
If you're crazy or just immature
She's simply astounded
That you're still dumbfounded
Or maybe a bit insecure.

It's probably in there somewhere
And could be replayed if you dare
You ought to go find it
And try to rewind it
And put some compassion in there.

It's probably in there somewhere.
Down under her sea of despair
You ought to go find her
And try to remind her
Of the love you both wanted to share.

The Bipolar Blues

I wake up in the morning and I stare my coffee down
I look out at the world and wonder, why?
I have my daily dose of doubt, washed down with deep regret
And think about my life, then start to cry.

A grown man shouldn't act like this or put it in a song
It doesn't do me much good anyway.
I shake it off and say a prayer, "I thank you for my life"
I wouldn't have it any other way.

Thank you for intensity that lives inside the grief.
Thank you for the rain I turn to tear.
The bottom's just an empty place that fits between the peaks
And tells you that a day of joy is near.

It Ain't Easy Being Old

I like the dating game
It's different from the mating game
They're similar except in name
But they're not the same.

I like a pretty one
And I like to have my fun
I'm just playing hit and run
'Cause my serious time is done.

So come on right over here
You ain't got a thing to fear
You can even get quite near
And never have to shed a tear.

I'm not very serious
I play at mysterious
I don't get delirious
I only get beerious.

The Pig's Eye Open Mike Subtext Shuffle

Schizophrenic dreams are closing in
Paranoid excuses seem quite thin
This doesn't indicate the state I'm in
But where I was at yesterday.

I think I'm quite alright now, but it's not a cure
Although I like you all I'm feeling insecure
The only thing it indicates is I'm not sure
Of who I want to be today.

Changes happen
There's things that I don't understand.
I was nappin'
And the universe got out of hand.

I've dropped all my defenses and I'm standing here
I've been drinking Pabst at one-fifty a beer
You can see right through me but I have no fear
'Cause soon I will be on my way.

Strange things happen
Things that I don't understand
No one's clappin'
But this is where I take my stand.
I think that all of this was planned.
But keep it up and I'll be banned.

The Enlightenment Blues

It seems the times my life went bad
Was when I thought I really knew
Exactly what would happen next
But really didn't have a clue

Of what was happening then
Just like I don't know when
This current trip will end.

My memory of the past has changed
As each catharsis shapes the feel
I filter recollection through
I doubt that I recall what's real

Except in terms of how
It shapes the way I plow
Through all that's here and now.

The current moment's fine with me
The past's depression and regret
The future holds anxiety
They both can only cause upset

To what is happening here
By planting doubt and fear
In what is new and clear.

Other Titles by Salem House Press

Ideas for America I~ by Matthew J. Frasser

The Ugly European~ by Peter R. Senn

Salem Secret Underground: The History of the Tunnels in the City~ by Christopher Jon Luke Dowgin

Old Naumkeag: Historical Sketch of the City of Salem and the Surrounding Towns~ Carl Webber and Winfield S. Nevins

The Pocket Guide to Salem 1885~ by Thomas Franklin Hunt and Henry Morrill Batchelder

The Answer~ by Hal Brown

www.salemhousepress.com
Facebook: Salem House Press

Will Pirone

Will Pirone grew up and went to school on Boston's north shore. He holds a degree in English from Salem State University. After spending much of his life in California, he retired to Salem.

Mr. Pirone has been writing poetry and playing music since childhood. They dominated his early life. As professions, he found them as political as government service and as competitive as business. So he tried both of these. In a life of writing monitoring reports, grant applications and business proposals, poetry functioned as a running commentary on an active and eccentric life in a chaotic and interesting time.

www.ingramcontent.com/pod-product-compliance
Lightning Source LLC
Chambersburg PA
CBHW031212090426
42736CB00009B/887